PRAYERS

of our

CHILDREN

CHARLES MWEWA

Published by:

ACP

Ottawa ON, Canada

www.acpress.ca

ISBN: 978-1-998788-50-7

DEDICATION

To

My sweetest angels:

Emmerance,

Tashany-Idyllia

&

Cuteravive

CONTENTS

PREFACE

My interest and motivation for writing this little book of prayers and declarations are twofold: First, my upbringing lacked a spiritual figure, because my father died when I was only ten. And second, my children themselves give me so many reasons why a book of this nature must be written.

In the summer of 2013, my family moved from Toronto, Ontario, to Milton, Ontario. My wife, Clarice, and I discovered shortly after moving that we were late to enlist Emmerance and Tashany for the summer camps available in the area.

We were faced with a challenge.

We could either send them to an expensive camp outside of Milton or we were left with no option but to stay with them at home the entire summer.

We stayed with the children.

This meant that we had to design our schedule not based on our individual jobs, but on the welfare and interest of the children.

Clarice's work, fortunately, was flexible; she could begin work early and knock off late, and vice-versa.

I had just started a legal business and adjusting to my own schedule was not a big deal.

It was during this time with the kids that I developed a true bond with them. I drove them to work; we had lunch together and they played games on the computer, as I worked on various files.

But it was also around this time that I began to give them Christian poems to memorize and recite.

Some of those poems make up a good chunk of this little book.

In February 2016, we moved from Milton, Ontario, to Kitchener, Ontario. Just the year prior, 2015, Cuteravive had joined the family. In Kitchener, I began what we called the "Mwewa Home Church." I spent about two years teaching my family nothing but prayer.

I believe that the first thing a father can leave behind for his children is love, and second, prayer.

Then the rest.

Prayer is not just a spiritual attitude; prayer has been my faithful companion across the years. If there is anything I wish to bequeath to my children, it must be prayer, among other things. I believe that if they can pray, they can make all things happen favorably for them. Prayer is the only means through which they can converse and communicate with their heavenly Father.

When I first wrote this manuscript in 2013, I dedicated it to Emmerance and Tashany. So, I subtitled the little book, "The Prayers for Emmerance & Tashany." With the arrival of Cuteravive in 2015, the subtitle should have read as, "The Prayers of Emmerance, Tashany & Cuteravive," with the change of the earlier preposition of "for" with "of." However, since both Emmerance is now an adult, and Tashany is in her late teens, and Cutera, shortened form of Cuteravive, is going to eight, I decided to simply entitle this version as *Prayers of Our Children*, because I have all the children of the world at heart.

My prayer and wish as a father and a human being is that they will grow up as God-fearing children who will know, love and understand how to access God`s presence for themselves.

But this book is for all the children of the world as well. That through these simple prayers and verses, they can come to know the love of our Lord and Savior Jesus Christ.

PRAYERS OF OUR CHILDREN

Bedtime Prayer

Dear Father, to you I pray
And I thank you for this day,
For Mom, Dad and the all world
And I believe in God`s Word

Now as I lay down to sleep
Let my soul your angels keep
All evil keep far away
Wake me again, if you may

In the name of Jesus Christ,
Amen.

Memory Verse: **Psalm 63:6-8**
"When I remember You on my bed, I meditate
on You in the night watches. Because You
have been my help, therefore, in the shadow of
Your wings I will rejoice. My soul follows close
behind You; Your right hand upholds me."

Morning Prayer

Dear Father and God in heaven
Thanks for this day you have given
And for the night that has just gone
Please bless all that needs to be done;

I pray let your angel guard me
That good and right things I may see
Keep all evil away from me
And that good to all I may be;

In the name of Jesus Christ,
Amen!

Memory verse: **Psalm 5:3**
"In the morning You hear my voice, O Lord; in the morning I prepare [a prayer, a sacrifice] for You and watch and wait [for You to speak to my heart]."

Memory verse: **Psalm 63:1**
"O God, You are my God; early will I seek You."

Prayer for Food

Dear heavenly Father
We thank you for this food
And with others together
Please make these your gifts good;

We also remember those without food
We ask that provide for the them too
That they may have strength and seek good
For You are love and true.

In the name of Jesus Christ,
Amen.

Memory verse: **Mathew 14:19**
"And he directed the people to sit down on
the grass. Taking the five loaves and the two
fish and looking up to heaven, he gave thanks
and broke the loaves. Then he gave them to
the disciples, and the disciples gave them to
the people."

School Prayer

Lord Jesus
As a boy of twelve years
You knew the Lord
And you read a book in the temple
Please, give me your mind
That I may have all wisdom
To understand my lessons
And follow my teachers;
Give me strength to know more
And courage to try new things
That I be skilled and know
And in life fly with strong wings.

In your name, Jesus,
Amen.

Memory verse: **Luke 2:41-52**

"Every year his parents went to Jerusalem for the Feast of the Passover. When he was twelve years old, they went up to the Feast, according to the custom. After the Feast was over, while his parents were returning home, the boy Jesus stayed behind in Jerusalem, but they were unaware of it. Thinking he was in their company, they traveled on for a day. Then they began looking for him among their relatives and friends. When they did not find him, they went back to Jerusalem to look for him. After three days they found him in the temple courts, sitting among the teachers, listening to them and asking them questions. Everyone who heard him was amazed at his understanding and his answers. When his parents saw him, they were astonished. His mother said to him, 'Son, why have you treated us like this? Your father and I have been anxiously searching for you.' 'Why were you searching for me?' he asked. 'Didn't you know I had to be in my Father's house?'"

Vacation Prayer

Dear Father,
I am now going on vacation
And I know that you are everywhere
So, be with me and keep me safe;

Be the driver and the pilot
Be the guide and the door-keeper
Be my key to the door
And keep evil away from me;

Make me enjoy this vacation
And let me make many friends
Be there when I return home
To share in love what I will learn;

In the name of Jesus Christ, Amen.

Memory verse: **Psalm 23:4**
"[Lord] you are with me; your rod and your
staff, they comfort me."

Prayer of Hope

I am in God`s hands
And my life is in God
So, I will hope in God
And I will not worry;

God holds my future
And he orders all my steps
So, I will hope in good things
And I will not panic;

God has a good life for me
He guides me in my education
And he knows what is mine
So, I will not be anxious;

God is my Shepherd
And I will not be in want
For he prepares a future for me
And his favor on me shall be;

In the name of Jesus Christ,
Amen.

Memory verse: **Romans 5:5**
"And this hope will not lead to disappointment…"

Memory verse: **Jeremiah 31:17**
"There's hope for your future, declares the LORD."

Prayer for My Parents

Thank you for my parents
And thank you for the presents
For the love that they show
And all things more;

I ask that they will live long
And will do you no wrong
For you will watch over them
To keep them from all harm;

I pray that they will retire well
With good stories to tell,
They will be in good health
And increase in wealth;

In the name of Jesus Christ, Amen.

Memory verse: **Colossians 3:30**
"Children, obey your parents in everything, for this pleases the Lord."

Equal before God

I believe that in God
All people are equal
That all colors are equal
And that all races are equal
Just as all heights are equal
And all weights are equal;

I believe that in God
All tribes and races are good
That all Whites are good
And that all Blacks are good
Just as all Asians are good
And all First Nations are good;

I believe that in God
All careers make happy
That all talents make happy
And all subjects make happy
Just as all efforts make happy
And all able and disabled are happy.

Memory verse: **Galatians 3:28**
"Because all of you are one in the Messiah Jesus, a person is no longer [chosen] or [not chosen], a slave or a free person, a male or a female."

When I am a Child

I want all to know
When I am a child

That there is still more
When I am a child

And lots to look for
When I am a child

To set up a goal
When I am a child

And work till I score
When I am a child.

Memory verse: **Ecclesiastes 12:1**
"Don't let the excitement of youth cause you
to forget your Creator…"

Make Me Happy

Dear God,
My Lord,

Please make me very happy
Give me a friend and a puppy

And when I go to school
Let me play and be cool

Let me also be able to learn
And to enjoy what I will earn

Let me share all my toys
With other girls and boys.

In the name of Jesus Christ,
Amen.

Memory verse: **Psalm 112:1**
"Hallelujah! Happy is the man who fears the
LORD, taking great delight in His
commands."

Sinner's Prayer

Dear God,
I want to invite Jesus in my heart
To be Lord and Savior of my life
For God so loved the world
That he sent his Son into it
That whoever obeys the Word
And believe in Jesus Christ
Shall not die in the spirit
But shall live in infinity
I do believe in Christ Jesus
Who died for me on the Cross
Lord Jesus, forgive all my sin
And I accept you today.

Thank you, Father, Amen.

Memory verse: **Romans 10:9**
"If you declare with your mouth, 'Jesus is Lord,' and believe in your heart that God raised him from the dead, you will be saved."

First and Best

Dear God,
Let me be bold;

I will obey my parents
I will use all my talents
I will study hard everyday
I believe this will pay
I will not be lazy
I will not be crazy
But I will be my best
And aim to be first.

In the name of
The Father,
The Son,
And the Holy Spirit,
Amen.

Memory verse: **Mark 9:35**
"And sitting down he called the twelve; and he says to them, if any one would be first, he shall be last of all, and a servant of all."

Good Gift

He is our Father
And we have no other
The Lord will give us
Through Christ Jesus
The best of all gifts
Who our sins he lifts
He is the Holy Spirit
By grace, not merit
And he brings full salvation
To the whole of this nation
Our God is King of kings
And he is above all things.

In the name of Jesus Christ,
Amen.

Memory verse: **Luke 11:13**
"If you then, being evil, know how to give
good gifts to your children, how much more
will your heavenly Father give the Holy Spirit
to those who ask Him!"

The Kingdom is Children's

Heavenly Father,
I thank you because I am a child
Like I am to my mother
Obedient, humble and not wild

And to all the people, respectful
So, let me be to you forever
A child, at heart and truthful
And let love be my goal, ever.

In the name of Jesus Christ,
Amen.

Memory verse: **Matthew 19:14**
"But Jesus said, 'Let the little children come to me and do not hinder them, for to such belongs the kingdom of heaven.'"

I Love My Neighbor

Who is my neighbor?
But everyone whom I know
And even the one I don't know
For they are all God's children
And he loves them just the same

You don't have my skin color
You are still my neighbor
You don't speak my language
My neighbor you still are
And I respect you just for you

My neighbor is everyone
And everyone is my neighbor.

Memory verse: **Matthew 10:29-32**
"'And who is my neighbor?' In reply Jesus
said: 'A man was going down from Jerusalem
to Jericho, when he was attacked by robbers.
They stripped him of his clothes, beat him and
went away, leaving him half dead. A priest
happened to be going down the same road,
and when he saw the man, he passed by on the

other side. So too, a Levite, when he came to the place and saw him, passed by on the other side. But a Samaritan, as he traveled, came where the man was; and when he saw him, he took pity on him. He went to him and bandaged his wounds, pouring on oil and wine. Then he put the man on his own donkey, brought him to an inn and took care of him. The next day he took out two denarii and gave them to the innkeeper. 'Look after him,' he said, 'and when I return, I will reimburse you for any extra expense you may have.' Which of these three do you think was a neighbor to the man who fell into the hands of robbers? The expert in the law replied, 'The one who had mercy on him.' Jesus told him, 'Go and do likewise.'"

I Have Rights

I am a child, a little doe
And in the sight of Jesus,
Precious
I am not a toy,
Or simply a thing
I have a soul,
And in the name of Jesus
I have a place in heaven
So, treat me well,
And respect my rights
Because as I am
So is God's Kingdom.
Don't touch me in a bad way
But respect my body.
I may give up my right
Only for something right.

Memory verse: **Psalm 127:3**
"Children are a heritage from the Lord…"

Only One God

There is only One God
Only one creator, one Lord

I know he made me
I am happy and I see

He made my dad
And for that I am glad

He also made my mommy
Who carried me in her tummy

Everything around
And the earth is round

Were made by God above
For he made all for love.

In the name of Jesus Christ,
Amen.

Memory verse: **Deuteronomy 6:3-4**
"O [people], you should listen and be careful
to do it, that it may be well with you and that

you may multiply greatly, just as the LORD, the God of your fathers, has promised you, in a land flowing with milk and honey. Hear, O [people], The LORD is our God, the LORD is one! 'You shall love the LORD your God with all your heart and with all your soul and with all your might.'"

One Commandment

God gave one commandment only
To love God, and also my family
They are not two but one thing
Because when you love the King
You also love his kingdom
And this is real freedom;
The second is also like the first
And this is the very best of best
To love everyone, I come across
For Jesus died for all on the cross.

Memory verse: **Matthew 22:37-40**
"'Love the Lord your God with all your heart
and with all your soul and with all your mind.'
This is the first and greatest commandment.
And the second is like it: 'Love your neighbor
as yourself.' All the Law and the Prophets hang
on these two commandments."

I Belong to God

I am of God
I do not belong here
I am from above
I belong to the Father

I am of God
I am not of this world
Though I live here on earth
I look forward for heaven

I am of God
I am not of sin
I obey God
I long to do his will

I am of God
I am happy to be his
I am made in his image
I am what he says I am

Memory verse: **John 17: 15-17**
"I do not ask You to take them out of the world, but to keep them from the evil one. They are not of the world, even as I am not of the world. Sanctify them in the truth; Your word is truth."

I Praise Only God

I praise you my God
For there is no-one like you
You are beautiful
You are faithful
And you are full of good things.

I have heard of other super people
But you are my only super God
Because you created everything
And with your words
You made the heaven and earth;

In you Lord, I put my trust
Let me praise you from my childhood
Let me continue in my youth
And even as I grow older
Let me be a child at heart;

I praise you, O how sweet
I adore you, O how cute.

Memory verse: **Psalm 8:2**
"From the mouths of children and nursing babies you have ordained praise on account of your adversaries, so that you might put an end to the vindictive enemy."

ABOUT THE AUTHOR

Best Selling Author, Charles Mwewa (LLB; BA Law; BA Ed; LLM), is a prolific researcher, poet, novelist, lawyer, law professor and Christian apologist and intercessor. Mwewa has written no less than 73 books and counting in every genre and has exhibited his works at prestigious expos like the Ottawa International Book Expo and is the winner of the Coppa Awards for his signature publication, *Zambia: Struggles of My People.*

SELECTED BOOKS BY THIS AUTHOR

1. *ZAMBIA: Struggles of My People (First and Second Editions)*
2. *10 FINANCIAL & WEALTH ATTITUDES TO AVOID*
3. *10 STRATEGIES TO DEFEAT STRESS AND DEPRESSION: Creating an Internal Safeguard against Stress and Depression*
4. *100+ REASONS TO READ BOOKS*
5. *A CASE FOR AFRICA?S LIBERTY: The Synergistic Transformation of Africa and the West into First-World Partnerships*
6. *A PANDEMIC POETRY, COVID-19*
7. *ALLERGIC TO CORRUPTION: The Legacy of President Michael Sata of Zambia*
8. *BOOK ABOUT SOMETHING: On Ultimate Purpose*
9. *CAMPAIGN FOR AFRICA: A Provocative Crusade for the Economic and Humanitarian Decolonization of Africa*
10. *CHAMPIONS: Application of Common Sense and Biblical Motifs to Succeed in Both Worlds*
11. *CORONAVIRUS PRAYERS*
12. *HH IS THE RIGHT MAN FOR ZAMBIA: And Other Acclaimed Articles on Zambia and Africa*
13. *I BOW: 3500 Prayer Lines of Inspiration & Intercession from the Heart: Volume One*
14. *INTERUNIVERSALISM IN A NUTSHELL: For Iranian Refugee Claimants*
15. *LAW & GRACE: An Expository Study in the Rudiments of Sin and Truth*
16. *LAWS OF INFLUENCE: 7even Lessons in Transformational Leadership*

INDEX

www.ingramcontent.com/pod-product-compliance
Lightning Source LLC
Chambersburg PA
CBHW060626030426
42337CB00018B/3211